Thirlmere

Before the dam

Ian Hall

Published by Orchard House Books 2021

Orchard House Books
Raven Lane
Applethwaite
Keswick
CA12 4PN

The right of Ian Hall to be identified as the author of this work has been asserted by him in accordance with the Copyright, Design and Patents Act 1988

A CIP catalogue record is available from the British Library

Copyright © 2021 Ian Hall
All rights reserved
ISBN: 9798752570827
www.orchardhousebooks.co.uk

Front cover

The front cover is one of very many paintings of the iconic Wath Bridges which crossed the narrow waist between the twin lakes. This one hangs in Mirehouse and is used by kind permission of the Spedding family. Had Thirlmere not been flooded these bridges would be as frequently photographed as Ashness Bridge is today, and Thirlmere as much a balm to the soul as Derwentwater.

Dedication

To Jennifer, in celebration of fifty years of marriage.

The Virgin Valley

William Taylor Longmire

This first painting of the jaws of Thirlmere shows both its beauty and its vulnerability. The Victorians had only to build a dam just 857 feet across the little gap below Great How, where the river just shows, and sixty feet high, to drown virtually the entire virgin valley. They transformed a quintessential Lake District Valley with a pair of sparkling little lakes, spanned at their join by an iconic set of three footbridges into a barren reservoir providing the ever-thirsty 'cottonopolis', Manchester, with 50,000,000 gallons of water per day.

Wythburn was a productive valley, supporting several thousand sheep, fifteen farms, a village shop and Post Office, two Inns, a couple of lead mines and assorted trades such as blacksmith, cobbler, joiner – and of course its own parson. The church for centuries was a 'chapel of ease' where parishioners could hold ordinary Sunday services and also baptise their children, but for weddings and funerals they had to go the seven miles to Crosthwaite, the 'mother church'. The parson in the period we are covering (1849 – 1892) was Basil Ranaldson Lawson, and his story and that of the parish intertwine.

Thirlmere before the dam

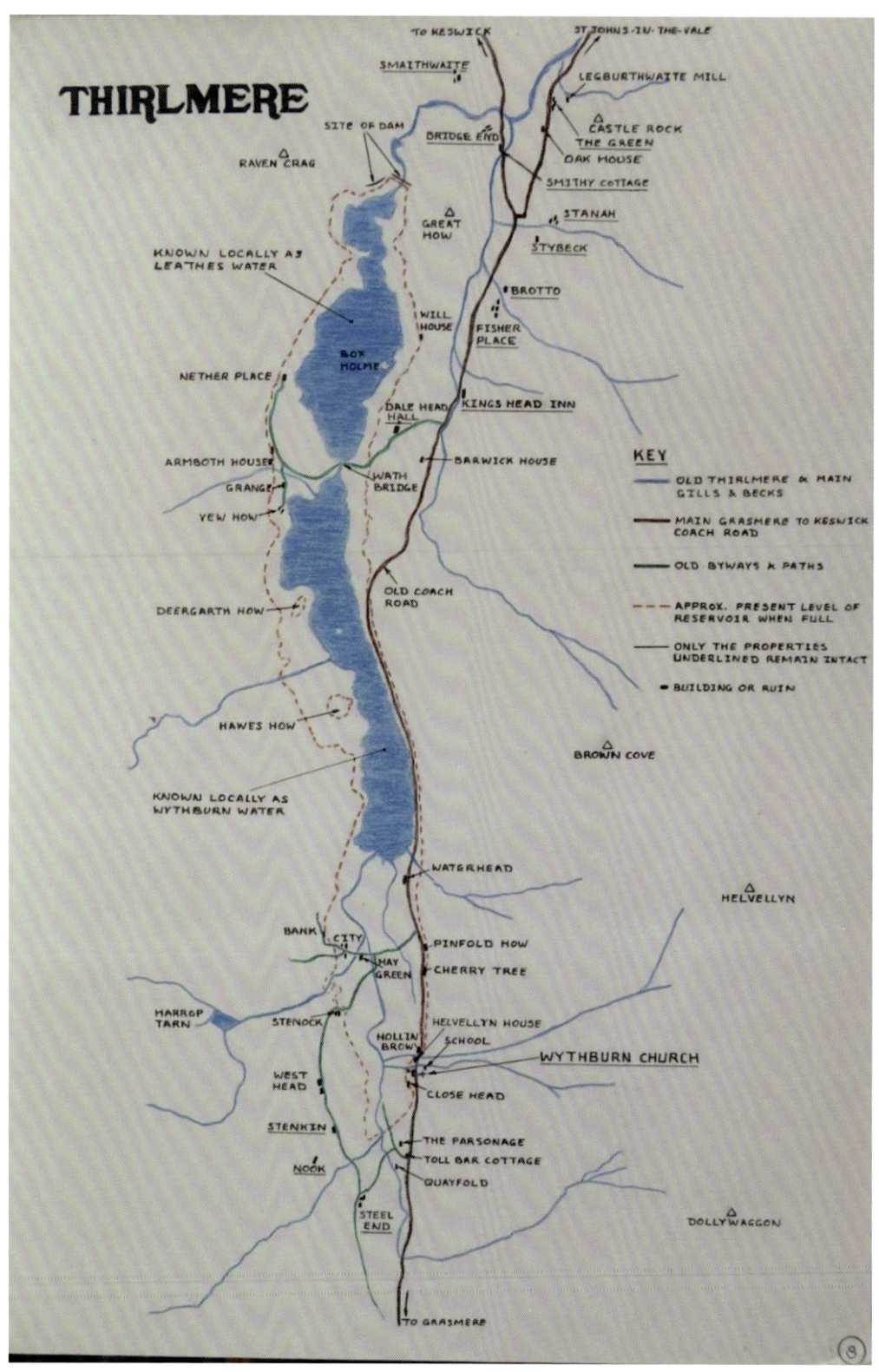

Map by Steve Rycroft

The Twin Lakes

This early Abraham Brothers' picture from the top of Launchy Gill captures the pastoral beauty of the Virgin Valley. Looking due North the first lake was called Wythburn Water, the second Leathes Water. The 'Wath Bridges' and a ford crossed the waist between the lakes, providing the only vehicle route from Armboth on the Western shore (left of picture) to the Ambleside to Keswick carriageway – the main entry point for tourists. Wordsworth and Coleridge regularly used to cross from the main road over these bridges to continue along the packhorse route down the Western shore to rejoin the main road at Smaithwaite.

Armboth

Painting courtesy of Katie Plumbly

A wonderful painting of Armboth House from close to Dale Head Hall which has been in the Countess Ossalinsky's family for over 150 years. Armboth was her ancestral home when she was plain Mary Jackson. We will learn a little of her history as we go along. Note the three small bridges, connected by a raised causeway to allow foot traffic across. There is a ford to the left of them for horse-drawn carts. To the left of Armboth House is Fisher Crag, behind is Armboth Fell. Mary became the Countess on her marriage to a Russian fortune hunter, Count Boris Vladimir Ossalinsky. She was soon rid of him, but kept her name – and lived up to its aristocratic pedigree throughout her long life: 1820-1902.

Parson Basil Lawson

Basil Ranaldson Lawson was the parson in Wythburn parish from 1849 till his death in 1892. He left two sketchbooks filled with drawings and watercolours of many of the Thirlmere farms and cottages which we will draw on frequently, plus a journal of his first four years in the valley. He will be our guide throughout, with his intimate knowledge of the parish and parishioners in the period when the old ways were changing, culminating in the building of the dam and aqueduct by Manchester Water Works Committee.

Since the photograph of Basil shows him as an old man, overleaf is one of his son, also officially Basil Ranaldson Lawson, but always known as Bazzy. The family likeness is unmistakeable, and it was more in this guise that he spent his early years in the valley.

5

Basil and his wife Elizabeth had four surviving children: Bazzy, Ellen, Henrietta Ada and Fanny. Whilst it is unknown whether Basil and the Countess were close friends it is certainly true that their children were. The Countess's son, Vladimir Boris, gave Fanny away at her marriage in 1892 as Basil had recently died, and was a witness on her marriage certificate. In the next generation Fanny's only daughter Ada was a close friend of Boris's daughter Edith, corresponding regularly and coming for holidays in Keswick from her home back in Barnardiston in Suffolk. Initially it is Armboth House which connects Basil and The Countess Ossalinsky: she moved out from the mansion in 1848 with her two children to live in the fine Musgrave House at the end of Middlegate, the main street in Penrith, and put Armboth up for rent. It took six months to find a tenant; Jane Westray and her son Jonathon decided they had had enough of being the landlords of the King's Head, Thirlspot, and took on Armboth as a farm for Jonathon and a guest house for Jane to run. Yes, there was already a healthy tourist industry at least in the summer months. Basil and his family had lodged with Jane at the King's Head and were happy to be her long-term guests at Armboth, where they stayed till December 1852.

The Wath Bridges

An artist's delight, these bridges have been painted
and photographed many times. Over time they
increased from three to six, and from simple and
rustic to something much more robust.

This early sketch is by the Reverend Basil Ranaldson Lawson about 1850. We will see much more of his work as we explore the valley. Indeed, he is the main source of close-ups of many of the farms, and was a well-loved figure in the valley. On the right is the track up to Dale Head Hall and the other coming towards us leads to Wythburn and the parson's church.

Before being invited to be the curate at Wythburn, Basil had been a prison chaplain in Leicestershire, a job he hated, and we can see his simple delight in his new parish in the four-year journal he kept from 1849 – 1852. He was to be Wythburn's parson for a staggering forty-two years till his death in 1892, just two years before the twin lakes were raised their initial twenty feet in 1894.

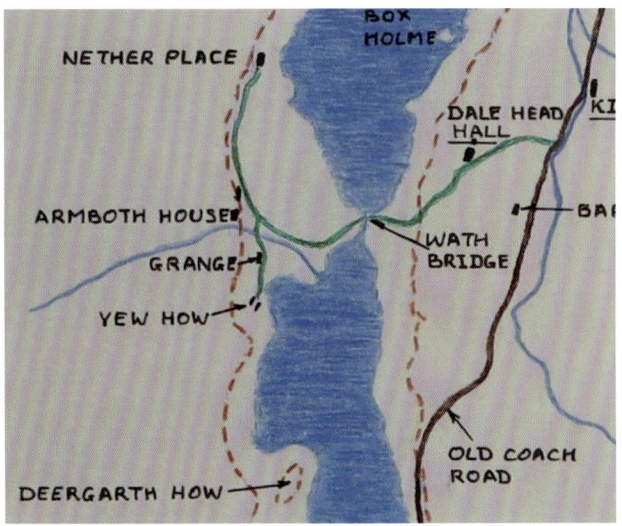

Because the Wath Bridges were so iconic, on the next four pages there are a few of the many paintings, sketches and eventually photographs of their rustic simplicity.

Thomas Allom, 1832.

One of the earliest sketches: each bridge has only one side barrier. The hill in the background is Great How, so we are looking north-north-east. The composition, including the fisherman and the rider perhaps influenced the next, anonymous, artist.

Artist unknown.

This beautiful painting dates from 1870 and hangs in Mirehouse, Bassenthwaite. Used courtesy of the Spedding family.

1880s: view from the east (Dale Head) side

Geoff Darrall collection

The three bridges from the east side. Armboth House is just visible in the background. The woodland was known as Wath Woods. The walling and sunken path are probably the same but the bridges have been renewed and there are now guard rails on both sides. Photography had come of age, and the image is crisp.

The same bridges from the west side.

Geoff Darrall collection

The bridges are the same, but the image is poorer. Nevertheless, it shows some key features of the Wath area. On the far side two tracks are visible. The ford is on the right here and the gated track leads up to Dale Head Hall and the Ambleside to Keswick road while the track going right heads along the East shore eventually joining the main road and so on to Wythburn. This was Parson Lawson's route to church during the four years he and his family lodged at Armboth House (1849-1852).

Grange Farm

Geoff Darrall collection

Grange Farm was just up the valley from Armboth House. It looked over the North end of Wythburn Water to mighty Helvellyn. Just further up the lake was Yew How Farm. From there on the track was no more than a packhorse trod until you got to the South end of Wythburn Water and the valley opened out to fields and farms again.

Basil Lawson and his wife Elizabeth lived at Armboth for four years (1849-1852) as paying guests of Jane Westray. She had been landlady of the Kings Head across the lake at Thirlspot and took on the tenancy when the Countess Ossalinsky moved out with her two children, Vladimir Boris the younger and Nathalia. By now Basil also had a son and a daughter. Just as Vladimir Boris took on both his father's names, so Basil's son was also the full Basil Ranaldson Lawson – known affectionately as Bazzy. Here Basil sketches the nearby Grange Farm. It's not often we have a photograph to compare with his sketch: either he is mean with windows on the back of the house, or more were put in between his sketch and the photo.

Yew How Farm

Geoff Darrall collection

Just South of Grange Farm was Yew How. This was the end of the road southwards on this side of the valley, and from here on it was just a packhorse or foot path. Hause How, a mile to the south of Yew How, dropped so steeply into Wythburn Water – the southern lake – that the footpath had to climb a hundred feet to get over it. The track that came through the ford at the Wath Bridges only went to the farms we have seen, plus Nether Place, further on from Armboth. From the ends it became just a footpath. Countess Ossalinsky owned Armboth and Nether Place at this end of the valley.

Armboth Sawpit

This, the third of Parson Basil Lawson's sketches, shows the old sawpit at Armboth. It is in a state of disrepair, but clearly was roofed – a sensible defence in rainy Thirlmere, where the annual average rainfall was over 80 inches (2 metres) a year according to the Manchester surveyors. Sawing here would have been a good wet day job. One man stood at the top of the pit, another down in it, pulling a long sharply toothed saw to cut trees into planks or posts. Every job in the valley was done by hand or horse.

Nether Place

Further along the track past the sawpit was Nether Place – another of Countess Ossalinsky's properties. I have been unable to find any painting or photograph of it in the 1800s: all I can offer is this aerial photograph of its place along the western shore, about 200 yards north of Armboth.

Aerial shots by Philip Wake

Nether Place ruins are unique in the valley – in that they hardly exist! There is no big pile of stones covered in moss, and very little exposed when the reservoir is slightly lower than full. This lends support to a legend in Keswick… that the elegant building on Chestnut Hill, now a nursing home, which is also called Nether Place, shares more than the name. It is said that the new Nether Place was built using the stone and some of the fittings from the old.

Jennifer Hall

Circumstantial evidence which may give credence to the legend includes:

The lack of ruins beside the reservoir.

The dates of demolition and building – the old was demolished between 1901 and 1911 according to the censuses, and the new has a date of 1904 on a downspout.

The new was built by Countess Ossalinsky's son Boris's widow, Sarah, and was lived in by their daughter Ethel till her death in 1949.

On the other hand, the facing stone here is dressed slate, though there may be rougher stone behind the roughcast. And would it really be worthwhile to cart stone six miles? Perhaps the truth lies in between: some of the internal fixtures may have been transported for nostalgia's sake.

Box Holme Island

Geoff Darrall collection

This little island just twenty yards out from the Eastern shore of Leathes Water, below Dale Head Hall, was the only island in either lake.

One of Manchester's 'selling points' for the increased lake was that it would generate two islands (Deergarth How and Hause How), and so clearly be superior!

Many Lake District islands are called 'holmes' – simply an old Norse word meaning island. Box Holme was probably originally Bucks Holme – the island stags would swim out to for fresh grazing. The mass of Raven Crag stands out in the left of the picture.

Alfred Heaton Cooper brings everything into closer perspective in this late Victorian painting. Box Holme Island is mid picture, and Raven Crag as ever stands guard over Leathes Water.

Wordsworth's footpath

William Wordsworth, his sister Dorothy and wife Mary, along with other friends and relatives, frequently walked to Keswick to visit Coleridge and Southey at Greta Hall. These old photos show their route – along the East side of Wythburn, down over the Wath Bridges, then along the West side of Leathes Water.

Manchester Waterworks Committee (MWWC)

Coming from Grasmere, over Dunmail Raise, the party would come down the winding track visible on the left of this picture, across the Wath Bridges and up the avenue of trees to Armboth, just visible on the right of the photo.

The large tree-covered promontory is Deer Garth How, now Deer Garth Island.

The rock of names

Picture by Harry Goodwin, 1917, courtesy of The Wordsworth Trust.

The poets and the ladies carved their initials on this rock face, part of a small quarry by the side of the old Ambleside-Keswick road. Manchester navvies blew it up, ostensibly to use the stone but more likely to defuse objections to its desecration, and the pieces for a while were stuck together in a nearby spot above the new reservoir. They have now been re-assembled at the Wordsworth Museum, Grasmere.

The names were on the clear face of the quarried rock, in a vertical line. At the top – naturally – was WW for William Wordsworth. Below him, in the sort of lovers' carvings still to be found on trees and buildings came MH for Mary Hutchinson. This narrows down the date of the carving pretty accurately, for Mary became William's wife on 4th October 1802 – less than two years after William and Dorothy moved in to Dove Cottage. Next on the list (ignoring other later additions to the left) is DW for Dorothy Wordsworth, and below her STC for Samuel Taylor Coleridge. Below him is JW for John Wordsworth, William and Dorothy's brother. Then, at the bottom, SH for Sara Hutchinson, Mary's sister and long-time idol of STC. Clearly there was a fair bit of artistic licence in Harry Goodwin's painting; but then, as it's signed 1917 it was painted long after the rock disappeared.

Photo courtesy of The Armitt Trust

The continuing path

MWWC

Once the Wordsworth party had crossed the Wath Bridges they would walk in front of Armboth House and on past Nether Place. The picture above shows the track winding along the edge of Leathes Water. You can just make out Armboth House on the right and Dale head Hall on the left of the photo.

The track is fairly clear on the 1863 map to the left.

iStock photos

I have traced on (in blue) what I think is the ancient footpath which Wordsworth, Coleridge – and many others – would have used to get from Armboth to the Ambleside-Keswick road at Smaithwaite.

The thin promontory in the centre of the picture is Otter Bield, shown on the next page as one of Basil's sketches, along with his sketch of Great How from Deer Garth. One Wath Bridge is showing.

Along with Parson Basil and his wife Elizabeth we will move now from Leathes Water up the valley beyond Wythburn Water to their new home near the church. One backward look at the lower lake, as we say goodbye for now.

This engraving by W. Banks and son, of Edinburgh distils the very essence of the lovely old valley.

Quayfold

Basil and his wife Elizabeth, along with their by now two children, Bazzy and the baby Ellen, left Armboth at the end of December 1852 to move into a farmhouse at the head of the valley, Quayfold. This is pronounced Whyfold, and indeed sometimes written that way, and shares its pronunciation with several other Cumbrian Quayfolds, Quayfoots and so on.

The family had been four years with Jane Westray in Armboth, years in which Basil's journal shows him enjoying country life – fishing, joining in the hunt, noting and sometimes joining in the seasonal jobs on the farms, hay time, washing the sheep and clipping, gathering in the oat crop. He is a keen walker, going over into Borrowdale, to Keswick, up Helvellyn and often to his favourite Great How, which gave such magnificent views south up the valley.

Geoff Darrall collection

The Lawsons at Quayfold

Occasionally Elizabeth joined him on these walks, but mainly she was busy with young Bazzy and, after the sadness of a baby girl who died at only two days old, another girl, Ellen, who she nurtured and raised. Ellen was just four months old when they moved to Quayfold.

Basil and Elizabeth spent ten happy years at Quayfold, their family increasing as first Henrietta Ada was born two years after they moved in, and then a couple of years later Fanny Eliza. Both grew up to be wives and mothers themselves.

On the left is Henrietta Ada, on the right Fanny Eliza, who grew up great friends with the Countess Ossalinsky's son Vladimir Boris. He even gave her away at her wedding, after Basil had died, and was a witness to her marriage.

The Head of the valley

Photo by Joseph Wright

This is a photo from around 1920, when the reservoir is fully raised, but I have included it as it gives a good initial feel of the positions of farms. Those in black were drowned when the level was raised in 1918. Those in white survived a while but were demolished as their usefulness to Manchester diminished, until all that was left was Steel End and the Church, beside the Nag's Head on the photograph.

The new roads that Manchester was obliged to build stand out starkly in these early days, before they planted a forest of conifers and nature filled in the west bank with willow, alder and silver birch.

Quayfold was untouched by the rising waters, as was Basil's newly built Parsonage, but this is 1920 and the new vicar living there was The Reverend Winfried des Voeux Hill.

Let's take a while to have a look at Basil's sketches of some of these farms and cottages, along with some very old photographs. We will go anticlockwise from Bank Farm right round to Waterhead.

Parson Lawson's sketches

The Reverend Basil Ranaldson Lawson served the parish from 1849 -1892 – throughout the peaceful period and right into the mayhem of building that heralded the coming of the mighty reservoir. He sketched many of the farmsteads in that time and the following pages give a feeling for those homely dwellings from a gentler age.

Liddy Hinde's house, Bank

Liddy Hinde was widowed in the 1860s and moved into this cottage at Bank, while her son George took on the tenancy of the farm there. She was just over eighty when Manchester first started buying up farms and land in 1877, and George at first refused to sell because it would break his mother's heart if she had to leave Bank. The smooth-talking John James Harwood, chairman of the Water Works Committee and chief architect of the plan to dam Thirlmere took to visiting Liddy, always with a packet of tea as a gift, and by promising she could see out her days at Bank persuaded her and George to sell their farm. Since the dam wasn't built till 1894, by which time Liddy would have been ninety-eight had she lived, it wasn't an onerous promise.

Harwood was a skilled negotiator and succeeded over the next couple of years in buying all the properties belonging to 'customary tenants' and the two big estates, Dale Head's Legburthwaite and Henry Vane's Wythburn. All that remained was the Countess Ossalinsky's five farms. She was to prove a formidable adversary!

Bank Farm

Geoff Darrall collection

By the time of this photograph Bank Farmhouse is bright and modern and of a style easily to be found in the Lake District. Nevertheless it is still just recognisably the same house that Basil sketched. In common with most of the photos of the old houses all the windows are wide open – perhaps photographers only ventured out in high summer. Somewhat indistinctly we can see a mother and her daughter enjoying the garden sunshine. The ruins of Bank are just below the new west road fifty yards north of Dob Gill car park.

Bank Farm ruins

Jennifer Hall

The most distinguishable remnant of Bank is this section of the old road which led along to the end of the lake, where it became just a footpath. Liddy's cottage was directly below this section, while the barn was behind the photographer's stance. There are huge mounds of stone, but it is hard to make out the floor plan. Nature has reclaimed everything, covering all in a merciful blanket of moss.

Lane in the photo on page 32

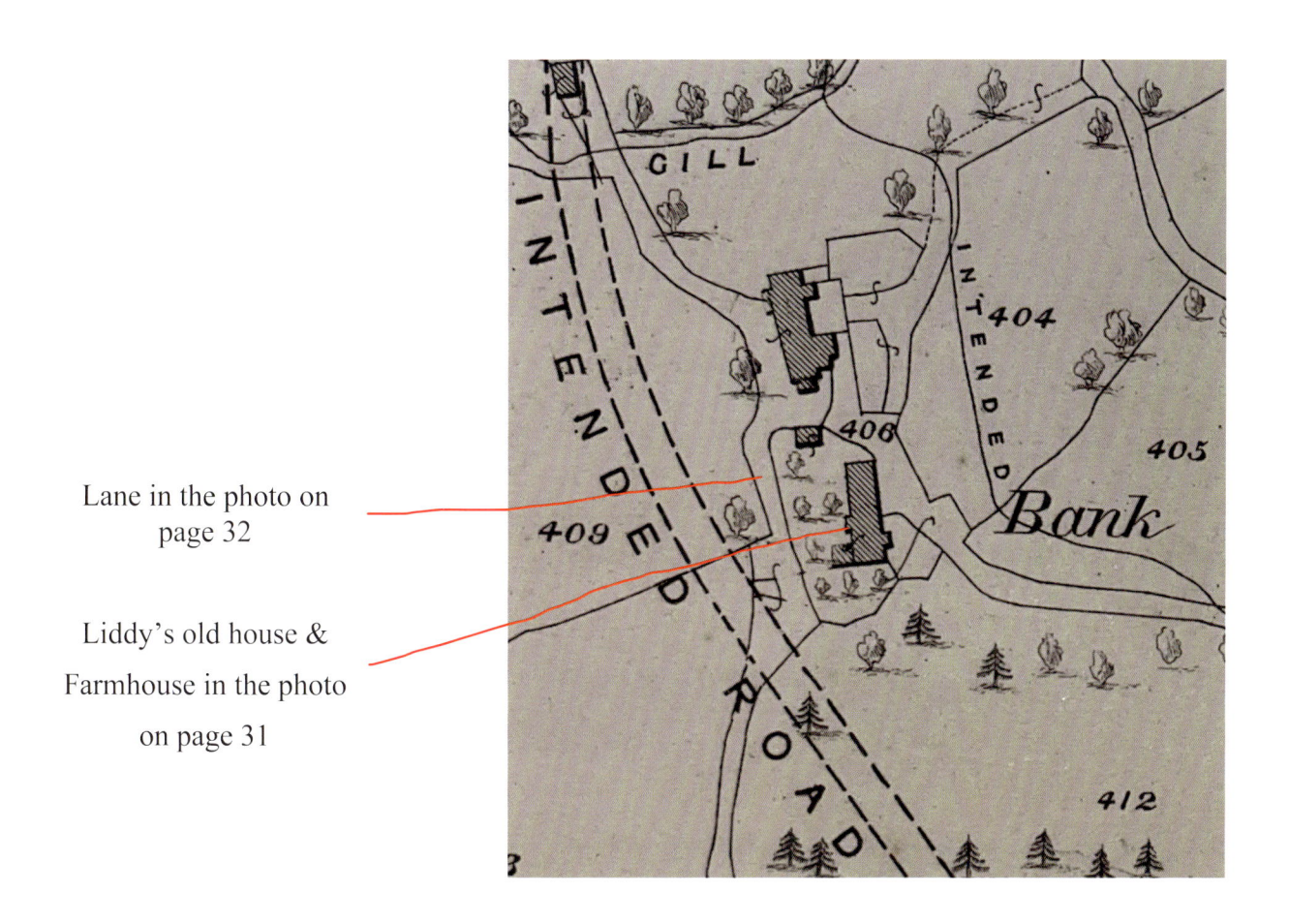

Liddy's old house & Farmhouse in the photo on page 31

On the next page we move on to The City and May Green, and a lovely Parson Lawson sketch of May Green. Below I've shown where he sat to make his watercolour.

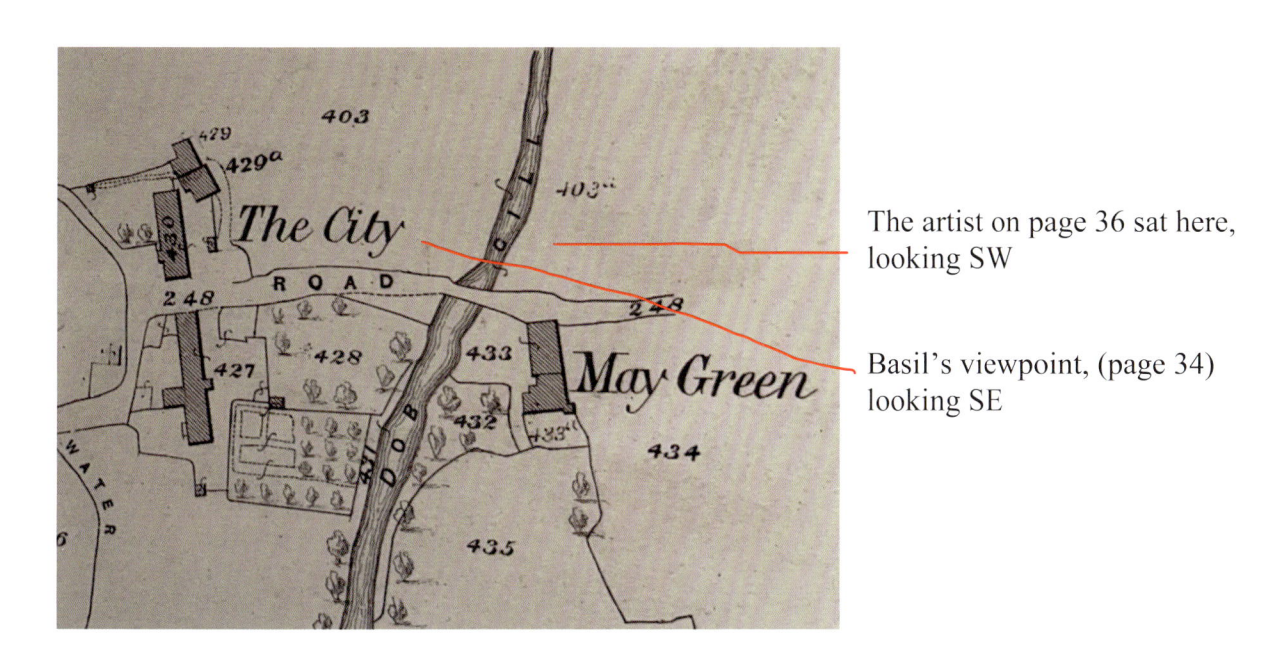

The artist on page 36 sat here, looking SW

Basil's viewpoint, (page 34) looking SE

33

May Green & The City

We'll move round Wythburn Water in an anti-clockwise direction. Having started with Basil's sketch of Bank, we now go down the track to the curiously named City. This was quite a collection of houses and the farm, and just across Dob Gill was May Green, another small farm. In 1851, when Basil drew this watercolour, a John Birkett farmed City, and another John Birkett was a shoemaker in the cottage at May Green.

Basil has labelled this watercolour 'Old houses, City, in Wythburn' – which in a sense they are, but the houses are more properly May Green, a small farm just across Dob Gill from the group of houses called The City. Dob Gill is running right to left, meaning Basil was facing south-east towards May Green.

May Green today

This photo from a drone on September 20th 2021 when the level was at its lowest shows the outline of the May Green cottages in Basil's watercolour. Underwater you can just trace out the remnants of the foundations and to the left of them the old road which ran from City, over the bridge (now a gap) and past the end of May Green. (Top is north)

Philip Wake

The City as it was in Basil's day

Geoff Darrall collection

A lovely mid-1800s painting of City from a point on the opposite bank from Basil's stance for his May Green sketch. This artist has emphasised the pack horse bridge. There are at least four cottages in the hamlet – one behind the closer three – plus a strange tall conical roofed building which could possibly be a pigeon house, where several hundred pigeons flew in to nest, producing eggs to sell. Note the white Bank house at the right of the picture.

Dob Gill is running down from Harrap Tarn, but in reality the artist has foreshortened the perspective, as will be seen by comparing with the aerial photo on the next page. Unless he has taken great liberties with the farmstead itself the large barn visible in the photograph on page 42 must have been built after this painting was created.

The City today

Philip Wake

This shot from a drone on 5th September 2021 when the reservoir was almost down to its pre 1904 level shows the remains of the buildings that were demolished then. The tracks which led up to the fell, to Bank Farm, and to May Green, are clearly on view. The top of the picture is west.

Still clearly visible in the cobbles in front of the main house is this mosaic of coloured stones giving the date 1871. This was about five years before Manchester officials started exploring the area with a view to a reservoir.

37

May Green

Road

Road to intakes

Cottages

Barn

Road to Bank

Old cottages

Rob Grange of Rob Grange Photography has generated this splendid image of how The City, May Green and Waterhead would have looked towards the end of the 19th century. Dob Gill runs across the foreground and under that beautiful old bridge figuring in the previous sketches, and we are looking almost due North. On the right are the lower flanks of Helvellyn, and in the distance the top of Great How. Behind The City the western track climbs out over Hause How. The farmhouse at Bank is just off to the left.

Bank and City in around 1903

Geoff Darrall collection

On the previous page the water is at its first level, twenty feet above the original lakes, and is only a little lower than in the aerial photos on previous pages. In the foreground is a barn and house at Bank, with the road leading down to The City – or what's left of it. There is washing on the line in the field beside the long barn, but little sign of a house. In the 1901 census there is a family at City, Edward Craghill, his wife Sarah, and their six children aged between one and thirteen – and Edward is described as a farmer, so the City was still functioning at this point. However, the water was raised a further fifteen feet in 1904, so City must have been demolished before then – not long after this photograph was taken.

Comparing the photo with the aerial shot of City the long barn is clearly the building whose foundations are to the right of those with the date mosaic in the front, which was the house. No house is now visible, so perhaps by now Bank has taken over the barn and the washing line.

Beyond the long barn are the ruins of May Green and it is just possible to see the road leading to it with the bridge demolished. Beyond May Green's ruins stands a bridge which oddly has not been demolished: it crossed the other beck that ran right down the valley, the Wythburn beck. The road led back to Stenock, our next port of call.

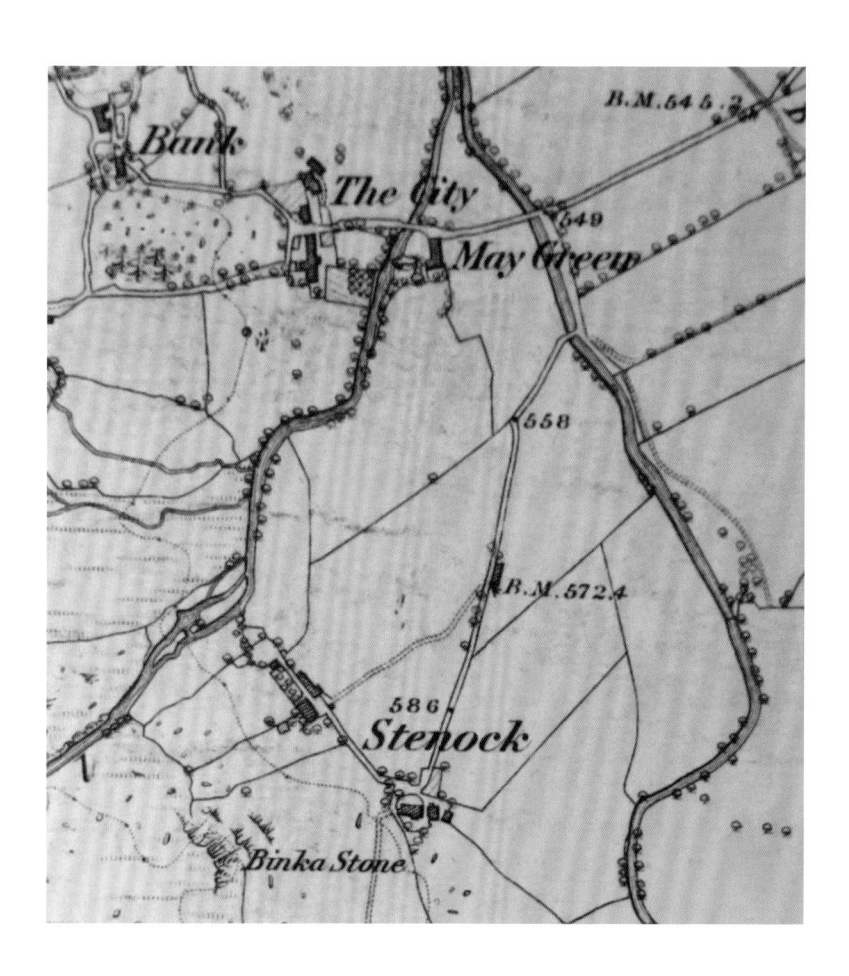

Stenock

Another of the parson's elderly parishioners was 'Old Nancy Dawson' who had a small cottage at Stenock, where her son farmed twenty-five acres with his wife Hannah. This must be around 1851 because Nancy was eighty-four in that year's census.

Again, there is a bank barn with a ramp up to it. The ruins of Stenock (or Stenack) are still clearly visible since it was never flooded. They are just to the lakeside of the 'new' west road round the lake, right opposite the 'Binka Stone' which is a striking stone face on a crag about a hundred yards south of where the road crosses Dob Gill. Perhaps surprisingly ruins which have never been flooded are a lot more difficult to interpret: the tree cover prevents the use of a drone, and in any case Nature has reclaimed the stones, covering all in a blanket of moss and saplings. However, the sheep-pens and the walls beside the road through are still complete and give a slightly eerie reminder of the lives lived out in this place.

Basil's sketches generally have an air of
dilapidation as in this second watercolour of an old
house in the City. The ongoing censuses keep
throwing up 'dilapidated' uninhabited houses. By
1861 Old Nancy is dead and her house gone to ruin
and the same is clearly true of this City cottage.

West Head

Geoff Darrall collection

This slightly unsettling picture of West Head with the woman framed in the upper doorway shows how big it was, with three separate chimneys. The ruins are still easy to find, with the wrought iron fence still there. For some reason the foundations don't seem as big as you'd expect, especially as there was a long barn to the left of the house above.

Buried among the ruins is this old range, once the heart of the house beside a fire that would always be lit. West Head was the last farm to be demolished, at the end of WWII. High above the new reservoir it was a noted sheep farm, able to take on the few fields left at the top of the valley.

West Head was the highest farm on the west side of the valley and even after the final raising of the reservoir level stood a hundred feet above the lake. For much of Basil's time as pastor it was farmed by the Gillbanks family, and it is clear from his diary that they were good friends – so good that there is a portrait of John Gillbanks in the parson's family photograph album.

This John Gillbanks was twenty-three in the 1851 census, and is mentioned several times in Basil's diary. He remained unmarried and is still there in the 1881 census, with his father still alive and definitely head of the family; his sister Mary is also unmarried at forty-seven. But by 1891, with the valley in the turmoil of hundreds of navvies constructing both dam and aqueduct the old man is dead and John and Mary have left. Basil too is nearing the end of his life and most of his duties are in the hands of his curate, Edward Hallam – as is the future of his youngest daughter Fanny.

West Head abandoned

Geoff Darrall collection

By the time of this photo (1943) West Head has been abandoned, and it was demolished at the end of WWII. These are the only ruins not either under water or hidden in thick woodland, except for the actual farmhouse at nearby Stenkin. There the farmhouse was demolished, but the buildings and sheep-pens retained for the use of Steel End Farm, which took on the noted West Head flock of sheep – and, so important was that flock, the very name, West Head! So now, what was known as Steel End is called West Head, and is the only farm or indeed habitation left in Wythburn.

The attrition of the valley's properties was slow and piecemeal. Manchester allowed many properties to remain whilst it needed to house workers, engineers, foresters and the like, but as and when a role became redundant another property would be demolished. The ostensible reason given was that the water needed to be as pure as it could possibly be, since there were no purification methods available then; but it is apparent that the city wanted to hide the reservoir away, almost to pretend it didn't exist. Forestry became a major industry around the valley, with trees allowed, indeed encouraged, to hide the reservoir from the increasingly busy A591 from Ambleside to Keswick. Dire warning notices appeared around the lake forbidding trespass in the strongest of terms. Wythburn slowly withered away.

West Head today

Philip Wake

This once great farmstead is a sad place today, with enough of the walls standing to remind us of its former glory. At the back, because it was built into the hillside, a yard-wide walled walkway keeps the water away. At the front old rendered walls stand forlornly while the body of the house is filled by the rubble that was once its walls. The neatly walled yard still carries its wrought iron superstructure, and echoes of the shouts and laughter that once filled it.

Steel End Farm, now known as West Head

Another of Basil Lawson's sketches, this group of buildings are the only inhabited survivors of the final demolition by Manchester, in WW II, when West Head Farm was razed to the ground. West Head had had a huge flock of Herdwick sheep, ably shepherded by the well-respected Isaac Thompson. The sheep flock were transferred to Steel End, along with the name West Head, and were managed for many years by the famous Ernest Brownrigg, who was awarded the MBE for his services to sheep!

Steel End today

Philip Wake

The houses to the right are recognisably the same as on Basil's sketch, but the old barn, the main feature of his drawing, has been converted to the pair of cottages above. The bungalow and modern barn are of course recent additions.

This farm and these few houses are the only habitations left at the Wythburn end of the valley, and Dale Head Hall the only survivor around Leathes Water.

Stackhow Bridge crossed the Wyth Burn taking the track from Steel End to Stenkin. Basil's sketch shows its artful curve: the abutments are still there 50 yards from the Steel End car park. Go down the footpath to the gate and turn right to the river.

The Parsonage

Geoff Darrall collection

Basil moved into the brand-new house built for him by subscription; the appropriately named 'Parsonage' in 1863. Sadly, Elizabeth didn't move with him, having died six months previously. Her death certificate notes that she died of an 'apoplexy', taking ten minutes to die, and that she was pregnant at the time. She was only thirty-nine. Basil was fifty-five and had to face moving to their dream home alone, and bringing up four children aged seven to fourteen without their mother. For a man used to having lots of time for his own pleasures and his ministry this must have been difficult indeed, and it is no surprise that he married again just two years later.

His new wife was herself a widow, with no children of her own, so it must also have been quite a challenge for her to take her place in the new Parsonage. She was Ann Clewley, née Baker, and a childhood friend of Elizabeth's from the same Leicestershire town, Barlestone. She and Basil married in Wythburn Church on February 22nd, 1865; Basil's friend John Tatham, vicar of Rydal, officiating.

Theirs was only the sixth marriage to be held in Wythburn Church, as it had been a 'chapel of ease' of St. Kentigern's, Crosthwaite, until 1863 when at last it was allowed to conduct weddings and funerals. It must have seemed a cruel twist of fate for Basil to have to bury Elizabeth at neighbouring St. John's in the Vale – the last of the Wythburn dead to need to be buried there.

Wythburn Church was not to enjoy the luxury of its own graveyard for long, however, as Manchester quickly judged that to have dead bodies so near the new reservoir was unhygienic. The graveyard was formally closed in 1938, and remains one of the least crowded in the county. There were 108 interments in the seventy-five years it was open – Basil's own being one of them.

Jennifer Hall

Toll Bar and the Ambleside-Keswick road

Geoff Darrall collection

Here we see The Parsonage in context, tucked in behind the old Toll Bar Cottage on the left above, with its own entrance from the Ambleside-Keswick road – previously a turnpike. It's a very short and easy walk for Basil to get to the church (far right) – or indeed to the pub. The building opposite the church is the Horse's Head Inn, later known as the Nag's Head, a famous watering hole for the coach parties of tourists who were coming long before Basil was in post.

Wythburn Hamlet: inn, church, farm

Geoff Darrall collection

The Bainbridge family ran the Nag's head for some years after the reservoir had been filled to its final depth in 1916. This photograph commemorates the end of Low Horse Close farm: the workmen are closing off what had for centuries been its entrance at the south end of the inn. With the reservoir now taking all the fertile lower pastures the farms could no longer function and one by one, as Manchester found it had no use for their accommodation, they were pulled down and left for nature to reclaim their sites. The Nag's Head itself survived until the 1930s before it too was demolished as Manchester sought to reduce possible pollution of the waters. Tourists from then on were actively discouraged with 'Keep Out' notices in the sternest of language being erected around the reservoir.

Even in the summer season the ladies on this coach need blankets over their legs, and the gents are well muffled in greatcoats. No doubt an hour or two's break in the Nag's Head will fortify them against the cold. The churchyard wall was whitewashed in those days – I wonder how long it took all to wear off, for it's the same wall now, but without a trace of white.

No doubt also they will spend a few minutes in the church remembering Wordsworth's description of it as 'This modest house of prayer'.

Inside they will see the tribute to the Rev'd Basil Ranaldson Lawson on the three West windows. The tribute which runs across the bottom of all three reads 'Erected to Rev B.R.Lawson, Vicar of Wythburn, a token of love and esteem from many friends and parishioners, August 1888. Glory to God'

Jennifer Hall

This is not Wythburn's only tribute to their well-beloved vicar. In the centre of the new apse, constructed in the 1870s, is a stained-glass window replacing the earlier clear one, again dedicated to Basil Lawson, posthumously. It was created by the celebrated artist and glass designer Henry Holiday who made the fine East window in St. John's Church, Keswick.

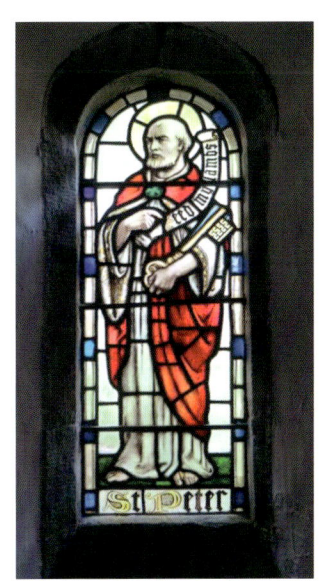

Jennifer Hall

The other two windows in the apse, shown above, depict David, the shepherd king, and St. Peter, the fisherman. These appropriate images were designed and made by the glass worker Hugh Arnold in 1906.

59

Looking across the valley

Geoff Darrall collection

This fine old photograph shows Wythburn and the head of the valley in all its unspoilt glory. In the foreground is the schoolroom and behind it the schoolhouse chimney is smoking. To its left the church is showing off its curved apse to good effect, while across the road the Nag's Head also has a fire on. Just behind it is Low Horse Close farm, with its big barn clearly visible. On the right well up the fellside across the valley stands mighty West Head with a long barn to its left, while further to the left and lower down stands Stenkin. Each of the three farms has a fine big barn, and all are well cared for. However, there is a hint of the coming reservoir just visible going right across the middle of the picture: the new west road put in by Manchester can be seen, meaning this photo was taken some time after 1890 but before 1916 when the level was raised a further thirty feet and would flood the fields.

It is not always appreciated that the water raising came in three stages, and that in between life went on more or less as normal this far up the valley. In 1894, although the dam was at full fifty-eight feet high, a valve and sluice kept the level down to just twenty feet above the old lake level. The aqueduct was full size in all its built or tunnelled sections, but on the piped sections only one of the final four pipes was in place. This was to spread the cost of the entire project over many years, because in the early years Manchester only needed 10 million gallons a day. In 1904 a further pipe was added and the level raised another fifteen feet, and finally in 1916 the final two pipes were installed in the aqueduct and the level raised a further 15 feet. A little later the dam was heightened by 3′6″.

Even then none of the properties in this picture was flooded and they were allowed to remain in use for many more years, though of course most of the good bottom fields were gone. One by one, as Manchester had no further use for them, properties were demolished: the last being West Head in the 1940s.

Basil's watercolour of Wythburn hamlet

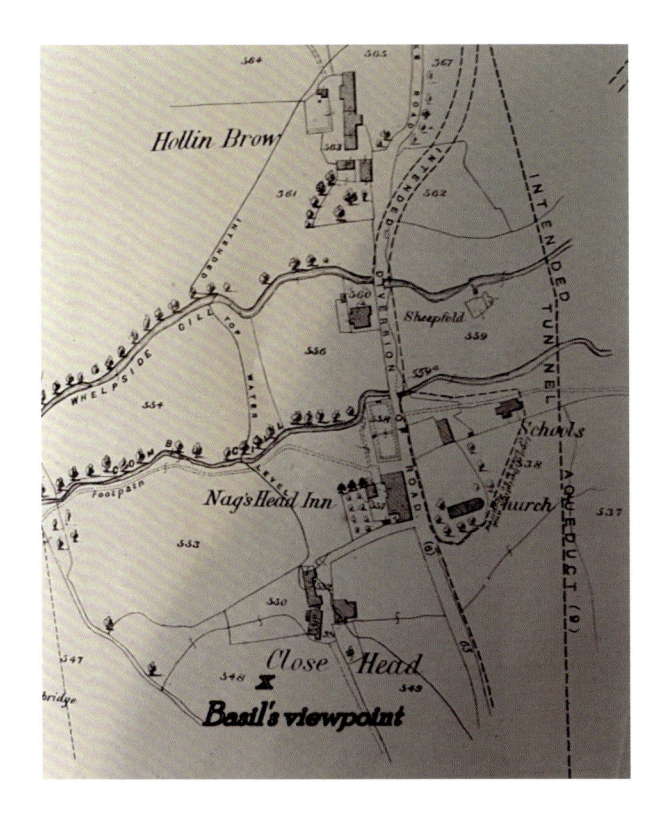

Note the graceful belfry in Basil's sketch, and compare it to the later version in the photograph on a previous page (p. 57). Manchester decided the church needed a more up-to-date belfry and replaced the old one as an uninvited 'improvement'.

There is a delightful story about Basil coming to church one Sunday to find the churchwarden astride the roof ridge, tolling the bell by hand. Asked what had happened to the bell rope, which hangs down inside the church, he replied that 'Johnty Hind had borrowed it for a cart rope and hadn't yet returned it.'

Overleaf is one of Basil's best sketches, this shows The Horse's Head and the church from the West. In the foreground is Low Horse Head Farm, (called Close Head on the map above.)

61

Horsehead I...
Horse t...
from

Chapel & Low
d Wythburn
r West

Water at the doorstep

The photographs I have of properties further down the valley from Wythburn all show the new reservoir almost up to the houses. Here is a selection.

MWWC

Here Wythburn hamlet is on the right of the photograph, and note that although Low Horse Farm's barn still stands the house has been demolished. This puts the image as post 1920, and the water is up to full height. The school house still stands, and to the left of it, on the left of the picture, is Helvellyn House – the last house built in the valley, presumably just before 1881, as it exists in that year's census, but is not yet inhabited. By 1891 it is home to three different families – nine people in all, all the menfolk employed in building the aqueduct.

Helvellyn House from the roadside

Geoff Darrall collection

The east road ran to the back of Helvellyn House, and here we see a mother and her son and dog posing for the camera. An early motor bike is parked, and behind the full reservoir reaches almost to the front of the house.

The old east road

In their Volume III for 1894, covering May to August, the Pall Mall 'Magazine' featured the opening of the Thirlmere Dam. This wasn't a magazine as we might understand it, but a hard-back book of some 719 pages. They did things in style in Victorian Britain. Along with the story went several photographs: I have only been able to copy from the book, unable to find a more original source, but they are interesting enough to excuse the somewhat poor quality of the reproduction.

Pall Mall Magazine

This first photo shows 'the parting of the ways' and is where the new A591 diverges from the old road just 200 yards north of Wythburn hamlet. The house corner on the extreme left of the picture is Hollin Brow, another of Countess Ossalinsky's farms. In the distance down the old road is The Cherry Tree, an Inn in Wordsworth's day, later a Post Office and Joiner's shop, and finally the home of Waterworks personnel.

For as far as we can see here the old road runs more or less parallel to the new A591, and in September 2021 was above the waterline almost all the way to the straining well. The following aerial shots follow its discernible track, in increasing close-up.

Philip Wake

This last close-up shows the ruins of Pinfold How, which usually housed miners who worked in the lead mine high up the side of Helvellyn on the side of Mine Beck which ran straight up from Pinfold How.

Mines Gill

One of the mines

600 yards tramway

Crushing area

Philip Wake

There were mines in Mines Gill for centuries, all seeking that elusive and valuable element, lead. When Basil first came it was known as The Wheal Henry Lead Mine – the company formed in 1837. Its major problem was that the mine was high up on Helvellyn, and any ore won had to be transported down to the road.

By the time the parish was building the new Parsonage for their parson the new mining company was building an immense 600 yard long railed tramway to transport raw ore down to a new crushing facility close to the main Ambleside-Keswick road.

It is a hard slog up Mines Gill using the old zig-zag miners' trod, but it repays the effort to appreciate the engineering and vision that went into setting up this industrial enterprise.

It was still limping along as The West Cumberland Consolidated Lead Mine when Manchester took over the valley, but lead run-off and the small amount of arsenic effluent always present were of course anathema to a water company, and the mine was, perhaps mercifully, shut down, having operated at a loss virtually all its life.

Hollin Brow

Geoff Darrall collection

Hollin Brow was another of Countess Ossalinsky's properties, a fine farm with two big barns as can be seen above. It stood about a hundred yards down the old road from Helvellyn House. The scar of the new A591 is very clear behind the farm. It was high enough to escape being flooded in any of the three increases in reservoir depth but of course lost all its fields and was finished as a farm, but Manchester Waterworks kept it on to house the manager of the straining well, Joseph Sandham, his wife and eight children.

Further down the old road Cherry Tree survived the first flooding, when the water was raised twenty feet, and indeed was also previously home to Joseph Sandham and his family. However, the 1904 raising by a further fifteen feet was too much for it and it was demolished just before the waters rose. The Cherry Tree as an inn was immortalised by a jaunty Wordsworth poem, The Waggoner, in which the waggoner, Benjamin, having resisted the delights of The Swan and The Horse's Head is seduced some half-mile later by the cheery Cherry Tree, which is holding a 'Merry Neet'.

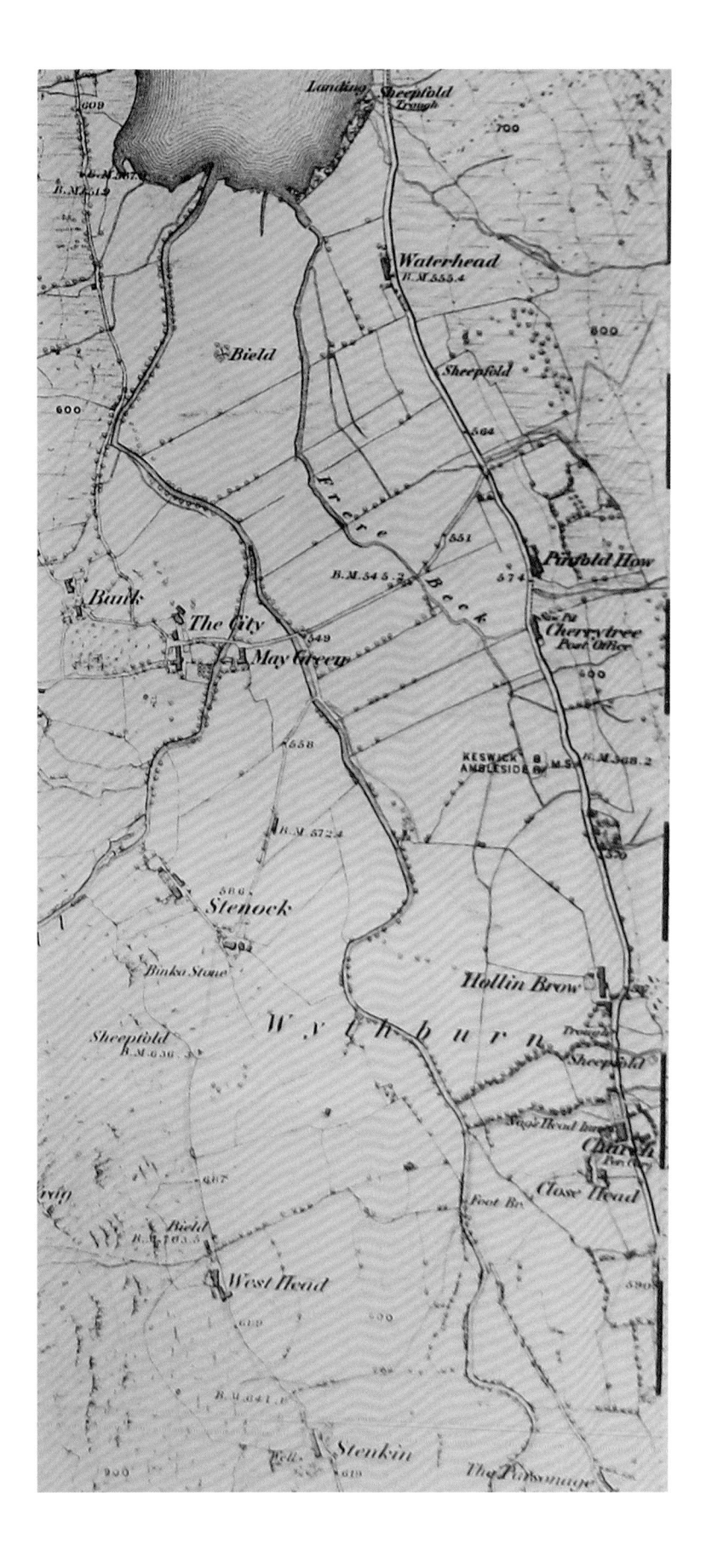

This old Map from 1863 reminds us of what was where.

Going north from the church and Nag's Head Inn, Helvellyn House is not yet built but Hollin Brow stands in a bend of the old road which slowly descends for about half a mile to the Cherry Tree, which hasn't been an Inn for many years, and is now the Post Office and home to the village carpenter William Walker and his family – as it was for over forty years.

A little further on we come to Pinfold How, standing at the foot of Mines Gill as it dashes down Helvellyn's flank. For many years it was home to miners who worked the repeatedly bankrupt and re-started Wheal Henry Mine high up the gill. The year-old twins whose death was the first commemorated in the churchyard were the children of John and Isabella Arnison who lived here. The stone is near the church door, just to the west.

Another half mile brings us to Waterhead, a small farm unfortunate enough to be below the road, and therefore just inches above the first twenty-foot raising of the lake.

Waterhead

Geoff Darrall collection

This is Waterhead Farm looking west. The reservoir is beginning to fill, and by the time it was up to its first level Waterhead was doomed. Note the new west road across the middle going up to Hause Point on the extreme right.

Geoff Darrall collection

The full impact of even the first raising of the lake by twenty feet is clear here at the front of Waterhead, with the waters lapping at the garden gate. Not surprisingly Waterhead was soon demolished and is not on the 1899 OS map.

This detail of the photo above shows a disconsolate lady and her dog unable to reach the front entrance without getting her feet wet.

In the distance we can just make out Pinfold How and beyond it The Cherry Tree – now no longer the inn beloved of the poets or even the Post Office it became, but just another house for Manchester Waterworks workers.

The old order changeth....

As we move on to the coming of the navvies, the machines, the dam-builders and the tunnellers let's just take a moment or two with Basil, growing old himself, recording various peaceful scenes from the old valley before it changes forever. These are from the end of the second book of sketches, presumably later in his life.

The delightful first view of the valley visitors would have glimpsed as their carriage came over Dunmail Raise. I love the way Basil has experimented with a few sheep on the top.

73

The fishing pool

This is pure Basil, with his delight in nature, the river and fishing. Many times in his journal he speaks of long lazy afternoons fishing with his friends – rarely catching much but revelling in the beauty around him.

The Parsonage

I'm fairly certain this is Basil's sketch of his home for thirty years, mainly because the specialised chimney in the sketch is the same as that on the photograph of the Parsonage earlier in the book. This is the penultimate sketch in Book Two of his sketches.

Countess Ossalinsky's triumph

Courtesy of Katie Plumbly

'What's in a name? That which we call a rose by any other name would smell as sweet'. So says William Shakespeare, but I doubt Mary, Countess Ossalinsky, would agree. She was born plain Mary Jackson; well-born, for a Thirlmere girl, the only heir to Edward Washington Jackson who himself was the only heir to Wilson Jackson, of Armboth House, Thirlmere. So even as Mary Jackson she was heir to a fortune, for old Wilson Jackson spent his working life in London, as a silk merchant in the days when the material was much sought after. He amassed a tidy fortune which he invested in property: in the valley alone he owned Armboth House and Farm, Nether Place, Steel End, Hollin Brow and Brotto.

Her father Edward was a successful lawyer in Keswick and he and his young wife Mary Banks cut a dash in the town for the short years they had together. Sadly, as so often in those days, Mary senior died bearing her second daughter and Edward just four years later, so Mary Junior was an orphan and the only heir to the Jackson fortune.

To paraphrase Jane Austen, a girl in possession of a fortune must be in want of a husband, and Count Boris Vladimir Ossalinsky had just the right mixture of Russian charm, roguish demeanour and debonair savoir-faire to turn a nineteen-year-old's head. Often described as Polish he came in fact from a small town just on the Russian side of the border with Poland – Konkorchkourovka – but preferred to be called Polish.

Armboth

Courtesy of Katie Plumbly

This wonderful painting of Armboth House from close to Dale Head Hall has been in the Countess Ossalinsky's family for over 150 years. To the left of Armboth House is Fisher Crag, behind is Armboth Fell. The road from the house crosses the narrow waist between the two lakes by the Wath Bridges, for pedestrians, and a ford for others. It fails to show Armboth Farmhouse, Yew How, Grange or Nether Place, but he who pays the piper calls the tune.

The Countess was born in 1820, married to Boris in 1839 and bore her only son, also called Vladimir Boris in March 1840. There followed in quick succession three daughters all called Nathalia – because the first two died within their first year of life. By 1843 Boris senior had left and the Countess had returned to her grandparents' home at Armboth with her youngest Nathalia, who was baptised in Wythburn Chapel on 24th September. With her grandfather now in his eighties Countess Mary took on the role of landlord of the Wythburn farms as well as more property in the wider Cumberland. Here she traded on her apparent aristocracy and was always known as 'The Countess Ossalinsky' and became a formidable business-woman.

By 1849 little Wythburn had become too small a pool for a lady of the Countess's stature, and she bought a fine house in Middlegate, Penrith – the erstwhile townhouse of the aristocratic Musgrave family, appropriately called Musgrave Hall. It took six months before a tenant could be found for Armboth, and as we have seen, that tenant was Jane Westray, formerly of The King's Head, and the Reverend Basil Lawson and his family.

In 1875 Manchester Waterwork Committee began to explore the valley with a view to creating a reservoir to serve the city, one hundred miles away, and to buy up all the properties – the three estates and all the farms owned by customary tenants – who had the right to sell their farms. By 1881 only the Countess was left, with her five farms and Armboth House.

Philip Wake

In this drone photograph Armboth House was beside the carpark of the same name. I have edged in white the visible remains of the road which came from the Wath Bridges (top left), alongside the wood which has since grown, and so along to Nether Place some 200 yards further on.

The Crosthwaite plaque

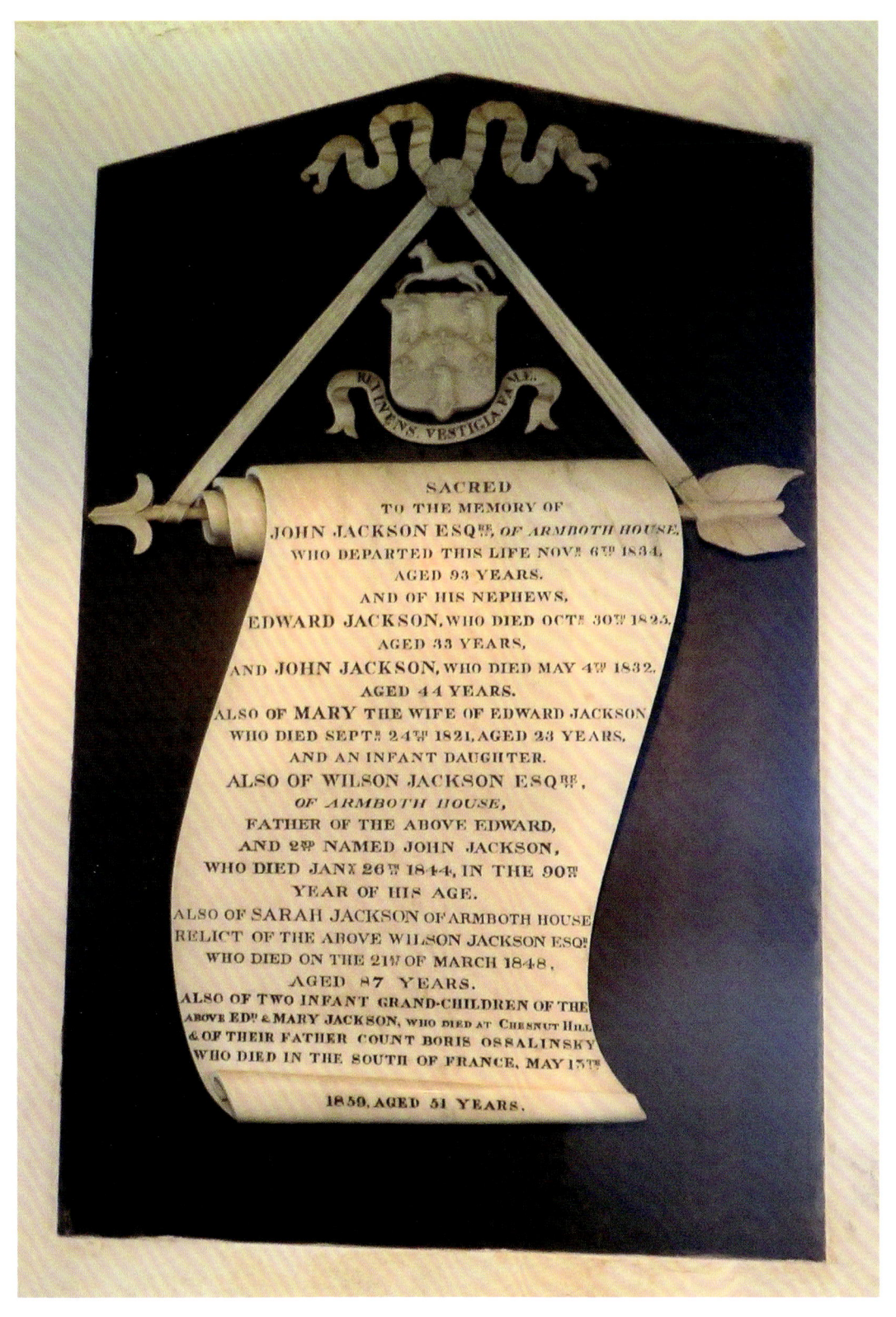

SACRED
TO THE MEMORY OF
JOHN JACKSON ESQ*RE*, OF ARMBOTH HOUSE,
WHO DEPARTED THIS LIFE NOV*R* 6TH 1834,
AGED 93 YEARS.
AND OF HIS NEPHEWS,
EDWARD JACKSON, WHO DIED OCT*R* 30TH 1825,
AGED 33 YEARS,
AND JOHN JACKSON, WHO DIED MAY 4TH 1832,
AGED 44 YEARS.
ALSO OF MARY THE WIFE OF EDWARD JACKSON
WHO DIED SEPT*R* 24TH 1821, AGED 23 YEARS,
AND AN INFANT DAUGHTER.
ALSO OF WILSON JACKSON ESQ*RE*,
OF ARMBOTH HOUSE,
FATHER OF THE ABOVE EDWARD,
AND 2*ND* NAMED JOHN JACKSON,
WHO DIED JAN*Y* 26TH 1844, IN THE 90TH
YEAR OF HIS AGE.
ALSO OF SARAH JACKSON OF ARMBOTH HOUSE
RELICT OF THE ABOVE WILSON JACKSON ESQ*R*
WHO DIED ON THE 21*ST* OF MARCH 1848,
AGED 87 YEARS.
ALSO OF TWO INFANT GRAND-CHILDREN OF THE
ABOVE ED*D* & MARY JACKSON, WHO DIED AT CHESNUT HILL
& OF THEIR FATHER COUNT BORIS OSSALINSKY
WHO DIED IN THE SOUTH OF FRANCE, MAY 15TH
1859, AGED 51 YEARS.

Jennifer Hall

When she came of age and into her inheritance Mary, Countess Ossalinsky, had this plaque placed on the south wall of Crosthwaite Church, near the door towards the east end. The Edward Jackson who died in 1825 was Mary's father and the 2nd John Jackson who died in 1832 was his elder brother. Had he not died without an heir Mary would have inherited little. The Mary who died in 1821 was our Mary's mother, who lost her second daughter in that tragic childbirth – leaving Mary junior the only inheritor of her grandfather Wilson and her father Edward.

At the bottom, somewhat cramped, the Countess has added her two infant daughters who died when she still lived at Chestnut Hill with their father. After leaving her, the Count lived and eventually died in the south of France in 1859, aged 51. I suspect Mary felt a tinge of revenge when she relegated that detail to the base of the scroll.

It is a matter of record that Mary lived either very close to her beloved daughter Nathalia (when in Penrith), or shared a house with her when they moved to London after Nathalia was widowed. Nathalia married a well-known Penrith solicitor, William Harrison, who, at forty-two, was more than twice her age. Before he died, less than a decade later, Nathalia had her own daughter, Catharine, and two sons, Anthony and Lawrence.

In London they lived in fashionable Kensington, at 30, Pembridge Square, partly on the vast proceeds the Countess was awarded in her battle with the Manchester Waterworks Committee, and their chairman, Sir John James Harwood.

Sir John James Harwood

Sir John J. Harwood.

Alderman Harwood was chair of the powerful Waterworks Committee and a skilful negotiator. By 1877 he had bought almost all the Wythburn valley, including The Leathes' family's Dale Head Hall and Sir Henry Vane's Wythburn estate. He had been lucky with Dale Head in that the squire, Thomas Leathes, died in that year, leaving his absentee elder son George to inherit. Old Thomas had been adamant he would not sell his birthright, but George, in Australia, had no such qualms and settled cheaply to Sir John Harwood.

Dale Head Hall in the 1890s   MWWC

All that stood between Sir John and the desired ownership of the entire valley and all its catchment area was one woman. As Mary Jackson perhaps she would have been over-awed and sold cheaply as her neighbours, George Leathes and Sir Henry Vane had: as the Countess Ossalinsky she had a well-honed gravitas, a veritable team of agents and valuers, and was the only opponent of the scheme to employ a Queen's Counsel. The Countess meant business.

All the other properties had been bought largely on an agricultural valuation – what rent was obtained; how many trees were involved; how many sheep and stints on the fell for them? The Countess Ossalinsky insisted that when it came to valuing her five properties another criterion must also be applied. Her acres were no longer to be agricultural, so that valuation was redundant: no, her acres were to be flooded and form a reservoir for mighty Manchester, and as such had a much higher value than the simply agricultural.

An impasse had been reached, and the law of the time provided that in such a case an external arbiter must be chosen by the Countess and agreed by the Corporation, whose task would be to assign a final value, to which both sides agree in advance to accept. The arbiter, reluctantly accepted by Manchester, was Thomas Huskinson, a valuer whom the Countess had used several times previously.

Huskinson's enquiry started on 10th October, 1881 when both parties had assembled seven independent valuations of the Countess's five farms, totalling 850 acres or thereabouts. Using purely agricultural valuations, plus a figure for the timber on her land, Manchester's valuers came to a figure averaging £24,000. Using agricultural values plus notional additions for the land's use as a reservoir the Countess's valuers averaged a figure of £85,000. Arbiter Huskinson had a difficult decision to make, and it was 29th October 1882 – more than a year later, that he announced his ruling. Alderman Harwood was astonished, not to say outraged, when Huskinson awarded a figure of £70,447 **PLUS** the sheep at valuation – a total of around £75,000. In today's terms this is around 8.5 million pounds.

Not surprisingly the law was changed immediately after this ruling, to become the Law of Compulsory Purchase, with very precise guidance as to valuations. Sir John quickly availed himself of this new law in all his subsequent purchases of land for the 100 mile aqueduct to pass through, so at least it was a valuable lesson.

Philip Wake

Dale Head Hall today – a fine hotel and restaurant. For many years Manchester Waterworks Committee used it for functions and accommodation.

Countess Ossalinsky's Summer House

In the light of this historic award it pleases me to offer a photograph of the only memorial to the Countess Ossalinsky left in Thirlmere valley: a tiny summer house built in her time at Armboth with her two young children, Vladimir and Nathalia, in the 1840s.

Jennifer Hall

Whilst the building may be small the setting for this one-roomed summer house is quite magnificent. It stands on a pronounced hillock in the woods behind Armboth and has superb views both up and down the valley. It is one of only six buildings left standing, along with Wythburn Church, Steel End Farm, Stenkin and Nook barns and Dale Head Hall. That in itself is an achievement. It is still known as Countess Ossalinsky's summer house.

Looking North the summer house had a magnificent view over Leathes Water towards Great How, temporarily masked by a stand of larch at present.

Jennifer Hall

While looking South the view was equally splendid, peeping over Hause How to Wythburn.

Uproar: Navvies and machines

The 1881 census of the valley shows a population of 150 souls, scattered around the farms and cottages. A brief ten years later the 1891 census shows 555 people living largely in huts, of whom 129 are women. Villages of huts have sprung up, almost overnight and all around is the sound of picks, shouting and gunpowder exploding. Here's a picture of the hut settlement at Bridge End, just below the site of the new dam, or embankment as it was called, to dignify its modern construction in concrete and stone, instead of the older earth dams. The new west road is clearly visible behind the huts.

MWWC

Deer Garth How Huts

Along at Deer Garth How there were just two huts, (circled in red), containing sixty-three people, the menfolk presumably engaged in building the new west road. Constructing the huts must have been a back-breaking job in itself, as there was no road beyond Yew How, seen here at the other end of the bay. The new road hasn't been started, but the Wath Bridges have been widened and strengthened and increased to six spans.

MWWC

Manchester's new bridges

MWWC

In order to be able to get heavy machinery across to the west side of Leathes Water for the construction of the new road, Manchester were obliged to widen, strengthen and lengthen the Wath Bridges, producing the efficient but less visually pleasing six spans shown above.

Constructing the embankment

Earlier dams for Manchester Waterworks Committee, mainly in Longdendale, in the Pennines behind the city, had all been earthen constructions. The Thirlmere dam was to be on an altogether bigger scale and with the huge pressures to be contained needed to be a concrete 'embankment'. Not only so, but its foundations needed to go down to solid rock, in this case fifty-eight feet – by chance, the same depth as the exposed height of the embankment would become. In all then, the engineers were building a 116 feet high embankment, to hold back a colossal amount of water.

The immense depth of foundation, fifty-eight feet, was dug by navvies with pick and shovel, although there is some kind of a steam machine, probably to pump out water, stationed on the intermediate platform. A great ladder on the left of the picture allowed the navvies to get out of the hole they had dug.

Considering that they were digging through non-secure material to reach solid rock the danger of collapse of the sides must have been a constant source of anxiety.

Pall Mall magazine

MWWC

Here we see the embankment rising above the ground level. The front is faced with blocks of Pennine gritstone and the middle is concrete interspersed with 'plums' – large blocks of stone up to three tons in weight. The dam is in two sections, east and west, because there is a solid rock hillock in the middle of the valley giving a perfect bastion for the centre of the dam. As the Bishop of Manchester, Dr. Fraser, remarked in the earliest stages of the idea "If Thirlmere had been made by the Almighty expressly to supply the densely populated district of Manchester with pure water, it could not have been more exquisitely designed for the purpose". This western section is the longer and is curved to give greater ability to resist pressure. Its foundations are nowhere near as deep as the shorter east section.

MWWC

The finished article

Philip Wake

I can't help but admire the elegant beauty of the dam, as seen from a drone. Note the handy outcrop of rock between the straight and curved sections allowing so much more security. The overflow now is to the extreme left.

Although the entire embankment was finished in 1894 (except for an extra 3.5 feet added in 1918), giving a reservoir depth of 58.5 feet above the original lake level, for the first ten years a lower tunnel carried St. John's Beck out just 20 feet above the original lake level, so the initial flooding was only 20 feet. At first the piped section of the aqueduct had only one pipe, allowing 10 million gallons a day, which was all that was needed. In 1904 an additional pipe was added, allowing for 20 million gallons a day, and the escape tunnel for St. John's Beck was raised 15 feet – as of course was the depth of flooding of the valley. In 1916 the last two pipes were installed allowing for a full 50 million gallons a day to flow, and the depth of the reservoir raised to 50 feet above base level. Finally, after WWI the extra 3.5 feet were added to the dam, making the reservoir as it is today: 53.5 feet deeper than Leathes Water was. The original area of the two little lakes was 330 acres; when full now the area is three times as big.

It may have been as much a political as a financial decision – giving residents, tourists and the vociferous opponents of the scheme time to get used to an enlarged lake in easy stages.

The Straining Well

This magnificent example of Victorian hubris looks for all the world like a sturdy castle, but is in fact the humble point of water collection and filtering before the water begins its two-day journey down the aqueduct to Manchester.

MWWC

This graceful superstructure stands atop a mighty pit, some 65 feet deep, all lit by daylight from the huge glass dome at the top of the tower. This allows water to be drawn in from the original top of the lake, 58 feet below the new surface. Until 1980 the straining well contained copper strainers to filter out any impurities before the water began its long journey – hence the name of the castle. Now it simply contains the valves which control how much water is drawn off – a variable amount dependant on requirements and the depth of drawdown at Thirlmere.

MWWC

The foundations of the straining well, going deep below the level even of the original lake. Note that the west road has already been made and can be seen as a line across the photograph.

The Aqueduct

MWWC

There were three methods of forming the 96 mile-long aqueduct to take the water to Albert Square, Manchester. The first, used immediately to get under Dunmail Raise, was to dig a tunnel. The men shown above are actually at the entrance to the second tunnel which took the water through Nab Scar, above Rydal Water. In all there were over fourteen miles of tunnels needed to get the water out of the Lake District.

Cut and Fill

MWWC

The easiest form of aqueduct was probably as shown above – cut and fill. The aqueduct was cut into the hillside and formed of a concrete U 7 feet wide and 7 feet high, covered over with an arched roof and the whole landscaped. There are 36.75 miles of this type.

The fall in both these types was 20 inches per mile – tricky with a tunnel and their range of instruments. However, such was the engineers' skill that it is said, possibly apocryphally, that the Dunmail Raise tunnel was dug from both ends and met to within half an inch in the middle.

Piped sections

The third type of aqueduct, used extensively to cross gorges and rivers was to use four large-bore pipes in an inverted syphon system. This doesn't require a carefully graded fall, as the water fills the pipe and can be taken under a gorge and back up the other side by its own pressure. Initially only one pipe was needed for the 10 million gallons a day, of a 40 inch bore. Eventually four pipes were brought into use to carry the full 50 million gallons needed.

These pipes are often carried across rivers and gorges on bridges, as below over the River Lune at Lancaster.

MWWC

The dam today

Jennifer Hall

The straight eastern section. Note the 3.5 feet high parapet added in 1916.

Jennifer Hall

    It's hard now to realise that this section of the dam goes down as far underground as we can see here above ground. Hard too to picture gentle St. John's Beck flowing peacefully here instead of tumbling out from the draw-off overleaf.

Harwood's memorial

Jennifer Hall

Alderman Sir John James Harwood, Knight, was the driving force behind the Thirlmere dam, from its inception, when he led the scouting parties checking out Thirlmere versus Ullswater, to the purchase of almost all the properties. He laid the foundation stone of the dam, and he it was who officially declared it open when the Prince of Wales was unavailable.

This is what we gained...

Philip Wake

The United Utilities complex below the dam. Now St. John's Beck comes out violently from the overflow to the right of the picture.

From 2022, not only will the reservoir supply Manchester, but is to supply West Cumbria with good clear water too. So at least now Cumbria has gained something tangible.

....And this is what we lost

Another lovely engraving of pristine Thirlmere, drawn by G Pickering and engraved by W. Le Petit. St. John's beck makes its leisurely way out of what was, without doubt, one of the loveliest valleys in the Lake District.

Appendix

For those who'd like to pore over the old maps of Thirlmere, here are a selection from the highly detailed maps and plans drawn up by Manchester Waterworks Committee.

MWWC

MWWC

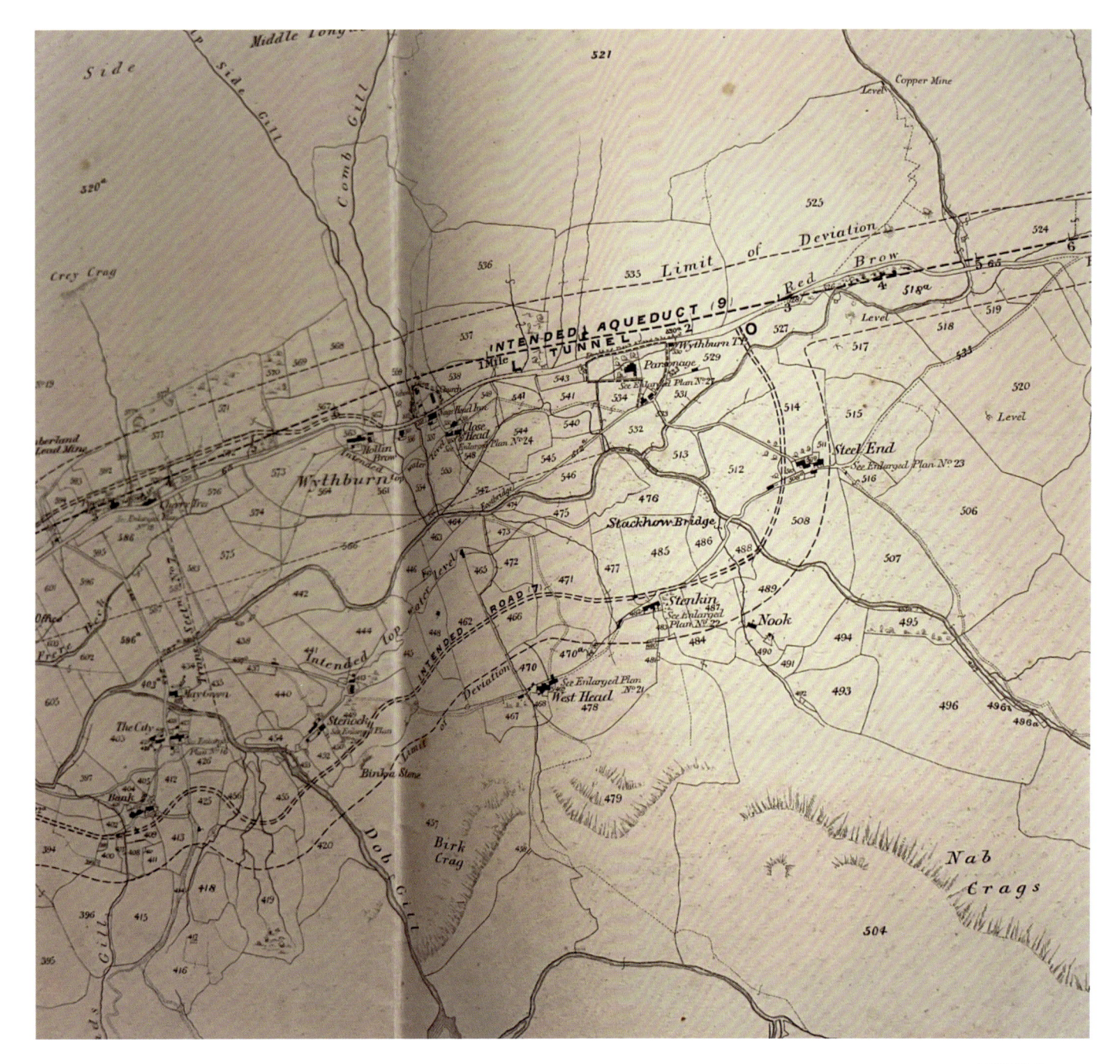

MWWC

Acknowledgements

My interest in old Thirlmere was first kindled when walking along the west bank with my wife Jennifer and coming across rather sad old ruins, covered in moss and under a canopy of scrub trees. I realised I had no idea of how the valley had looked before Manchester built its dam, and that probably the same was true of many people. The Reverend Geoffrey Darrall's book 'The valley of Thirlmere: rediscovering our past' provided many answers and indicated he would be a great source of both information and photographs. Geoff was immensely helpful and allowed me use of his extensive store of photos – each one used is acknowledged. He also put me in touch with Steve Rycroft who drew the splendid map on page two which makes it clear how much valley was drowned.

The book was initially intended as a history and Susan Appleby, who used to own a second-hand bookshop in Keswick kindly lent me what is undeniably 'the Bible' on the history – Sir John James Harwood's 'History and description of the Thirlmere Water Scheme'. I have held on to it for too long!

Margaret Armstrong's lovely 'Thirlmere: across the bridges to chapel, 1849 – 1852' alerted me to the remarkable presence and influence of the Reverend Basil Ranaldson Lawson, and I was lucky enough to be able to photograph his sketchbooks and photograph albums in Abbot's Hall Museum. This was deep in Covid days, and it was only under the kind invitation and supervision of Sophie Terrett that I was allowed access. Thanks also to St. John's and Castlerigg Parish Council for permission to use the books and publish photos from them.

Katie Plumbly is Countess Ossalinsky's great-great-great-grand-daughter and forwarded to me the splendid portrait of the Countess and also the picture of Armboth House across Leathes Water which gives such a vibrant impression of the valley before the coming of the reservoir.

It was a great bonus to be able to take drone aerial photos of the very depleted reservoir in September 2021 and I am most grateful to Philip Wake for his time and skill in providing such a fascinating set of aerial shots. He and I had a truly memorable afternoon working out the details of 'The City' and May Green in particular – difficult indeed without the benefit of a bird's eye view.

In the same vein of modern technology aids I am grateful to Rob Grange of Rob Grange Photography who hurried through the wonderful computer generated image of how the upper valley looked from a viewpoint South of The City, which appears on pages 40 & 41

Above all it has been a great pleasure to explore the surrounds of the lake both on foot and in a canoe with Jennifer, and all contemporary photographs not from the air are hers. Thanks for those, and the more so for the support and enthusiasm that has carried me along on what has turned out to be quite a journey.

Author's Profile

Ian and Jennifer Hall still live near Keswick where both were at school in the 1960s. They spent their farming life in Eskdale, at Fisherground, where in partnership with their good friends Geoff and Anne-Marie Wake they started both a campsite and self-catering business to complement the farming income.

Ian has written of those years in 'Fisherground – living the dream' again featuring many of Jennifer's photographs.

His years as a teenager on a farm in Borrowdale were the basis for his book 'Thorneythwaite Farm, Borrowdale' which explores the thousand year history of that farm and life in the valley.

'Every Mother's daughter' delves into 19th century life in North Cumberland as experienced by four generations of his female ancestors – a sort of imaginative history based on the actual women's lives as shown in church and census records.

He takes a more rigorous historical approach in 'Derwentwater: in the lap of the Gods' which charts life on and around that lake over the last five centuries, from the Earl of Derwentwater and his house on Lord's Isle down to the Marshall family's influence, including the building of St. John's Church.

Jennifer and Ian have two daughters: Catherine, a novelist living in London; and Sally, a Cumbrian entrepreneur who started and ran the holiday letting agency 'Sally's Cottages' for twenty years. They have five grand-children.